U.S. Department of Justice
Office of Justice Programs
810 Seventh Street N.W.
Washington, DC 20531

Janet Reno
Attorney General

Daniel Marcus
Acting Associate Attorney General

Mary Lou Leary
Acting Assistant Attorney General

Julie E. Samuels
Acting Director, National Institute of Justice

Office of Justice Programs
World Wide Web Site
http://www.ojp.usdoj.gov

National Institute of Justice
World Wide Web Site
http://www.ojp.usdoj.gov/nij

National Institute of Justice

Research on Women and Girls in the Justice System: Plenary Papers of the 1999 Conference on Criminal Justice Research and Evaluation—Enhancing Policy and Practice Through Research, Volume 3

Beth E. Richie

Kay Tsenin

Cathy Spatz Widom

Sponsored by

OFFICE OF JUSTICE PROGRAMS BUREAUS
National Institute of Justice
Bureau of Justice Assistance
Office of Juvenile Justice and Delinquency Prevention
Office for Victims of Crime

OFFICE OF JUSTICE PROGRAMS OFFICES
Corrections Program Office
Drug Courts Program Office
Executive Office for Weed and Seed
Violence Against Women Office

September 2000
NCJ 180973

Julie E. Samuels
Acting Director

John Thomas
Program Monitor

The Professional Conference Series of the National Institute of Justice supports a variety of live researcher-practitioner exchanges, such as conferences, workshops, planning and development meetings, and similar support to the criminal justice field. Foremost among these forums is the Annual Conference on Criminal Justice Research and Evaluation. The Research Forum publication series was designed to share information from this and other forums with a larger audience.

Findings and conclusions of the research reported here are those of the authors and do not necessarily reflect the official position or policies of the U.S. Department of Justice.

The National Institute of Justice is a component of the Office of Justice Programs, which also includes the Bureau of Justice Assistance, the Bureau of Justice Statistics, the Office of Juvenile Justice and Delinquency Prevention, and the Office for Victims of Crime.

Foreword

There is a common perception that the criminal behavior of women and the delinquent behavior of girls are not serious problems. Women are more likely to commit minor offenses and have historically constituted a very small proportion of the offender population. But these facts mask a trend that is beginning to attract attention. The dramatic rise in the number of prison and jail inmates is fairly well known; less so is that the ranks of women inmates are increasing much faster than those of their male counterparts. The pace at which women are being convicted of serious offenses is picking up faster than the pace at which men are convicted.

These dynamics make the papers on women and girls in the justice system, presented here, especially timely. What animates the studies is not so much numbers of offenders but the particular circumstances of the women and girls "behind" the numbers. The authors call for "redefining justice," the theme of the plenary session at which their papers were presented, to take these circumstances into account.

Whether justice should promote unalloyed equity, be blind to the circumstances in which crime is committed, and consider only gravity of offense and prior record, is still a matter of debate. In the current sentencing environment, the view of those who favor equity above all other considerations has won the day. There is another perspective—the belief that sanctions ought to be tailored to the specific characteristics and circumstances of individual offenders. Implicit in the three papers is the suggestion that gender is a special consideration warranting differential treatment. The writers amply demonstrate that women and girls who are caught up in the justice system enter it as a result of circumstances distinctly different from those of men, and so find themselves at a distinct disadvantage.

Sociologist Beth Richie argues that a key to understanding and responding to women as offenders is understanding their status as crime victims. Moreover, race and socioeconomic status, which also intervene at the intersection of criminality and victimization, need to be more fully explored. Psychologist Cathy Spatz Widom also examines the intersection—or cycle—of victimization and criminality, examining whether abuse and neglect in childhood promote criminality later in life by derailing young girls' normal development. She suggests that research could uncover ways to intervene effectively by examining aspects of juvenile offending that seem to be precursors of adult criminality. Judge Kay Tsenin sees the women sex workers who appear daily before her bench as "victims as well as defendants." For these women, she writes, justice needs to be defined beyond mere enforcement if the sex trade is to be dismantled altogether. She believes the judicial officer can play a role in directing these women toward programs that break the cycle of victimization and offending.

Research as a tool to enhance policy and practice was the theme of the 1999 Conference on Criminal Justice Research and Evaluation, from which these papers were drawn. The papers reveal the real-life implications of research for a situation of growing urgency. They show that studies have uncovered a link between the victimization of women and their criminal behavior and they propose that justice system practice can be enhanced if policymakers and the practitioners who operationalize their decisions redefine justice to take this special condition into account.

Those who wish to read more about the conference can find abstracts of the 1999 sessions on the Web at *http://nijpcs.org/pastconf.htm*.

Julie E. Samuels
Acting Director
National Institute of Justice

Contents

Foreword iii

Exploring the Link Between Violence Against Women and Women's Involvement in Illegal Activity
Beth E. Richie 1

One Judicial Perspective on the Sex Trade
Kay Tsenin 15

Childhood Victimization and the Derailment of Girls and Women to the Criminal Justice System
Cathy Spatz Widom 27

Exploring the Link Between Violence Against Women and Women's Involvement in Illegal Activity

Beth E. Richie, Ph.D., University of Illinois at Chicago

The understanding of violence against women can be broadened and deepened by focusing on the link between gender abuse and women's involvement in illegal activity—two of the most compelling problems facing contemporary criminologists. The groups of women who are most marginalized in society are vulnerable to both problems. A comprehensive response through public policy and programming can make a difference in reducing both violence against women and their growing involvement in criminal activity.

Violence against women: Extent of the problem

Violence against women—including domestic or intimate violence, sexual assault, and other crimes (for example, sexual harassment, stalking, and sexual exploitation)—has finally been recognized as a significant and persistent problem with severe consequences for the victims, their families, and society and has attracted considerable attention from researchers. The extent of the problem has been well documented.[1]

Domestic or intimate violence

An estimated 1 million women in the United States are the victims of violence committed by an intimate (current or former spouse, girlfriend, or boyfriend) each year, according to the Bureau of Justice Statistics (BJS).[2] Other studies estimate the rate of violence against women in intimate relationships to be much higher. The National Violence Against Women (NVAW) Survey, for example, revealed that more than 1.5 million women had been raped and/or physically assaulted in the year before the survey.[3] Another study estimated that between 7 percent and 22 percent of all adult women have experienced a domestic assault; and a recently conducted survey revealed that one in every three women reported having been physically attacked by an intimate partner at some time in her life.[4] Moreover, 56 percent of all Americans report that someone close to them has been involved in an abusive relationship.[5]

Morbidity and mortality data on the most extreme physical consequences of violence against women indicate that 37 percent of all women who sought care in hospital emergency rooms in 1994 were victims of domestic violence; of these, 28 percent required admission and another 13 percent required major medical treatment.[6] According to the Federal Bureau of Investigation (FBI), females are more likely to be killed by a spouse or partner than are males: 28.3 percent of women died at the hands of a spouse, boyfriend, or girlfriend compared with 3.6 percent of men.[7]

Previous studies suggested that women are abused by their intimate partners irrespective of their races or ethnic backgrounds. Although the overall rates may be similar, emerging research suggests that variables such as socioeconomic status, cultural background, and age may influence the impact of domestic violence.[8] Factors that include the limited availability of crisis intervention programs, the extent to which weapons are used differentially during an assault, and lack of trust in law enforcement agencies may heighten some women's vulnerability to intimate violence.[9]

There is also solid (although not as much) evidence suggesting that the incidence and types of domestic violence in same-sex relationships are comparable to those in heterosexual relationships.[10] Studies indicate that from 25 percent to 30 percent of lesbian, gay, bisexual, and transgendered people are abused by their intimate partners and that social discrimination and marginalization may complicate their attempts to seek help, thus increasing the risk of serious abuse.[11]

The consequences of domestic violence extend beyond the victims themselves. A national survey revealed that half the men who frequently battered their wives also frequently assaulted their children.[12] Other research has corroborated this finding, pointing to persistent intergenerational effects (for example, men who, as children, witnessed violence against their mothers were twice as likely to exhibit violent behavior as adults).[13]

While most of the research focuses on physical abuse, evidence suggests that emotional abuse also has profound psychological consequences for female victims of domestic violence.[14] Battered women are four to five times more likely to require psychiatric treatment and five times more likely to attempt suicide than nonbattered women.[15]

Sexual assault

Research on sexual assault reveals a problem of similar proportions. Between 1995 and 1996, more than 670,000 women were raped or sexually assaulted.[16] A report of the NVAW Survey revealed that 18 percent of all surveyed women age 18 years and older had been the victims of rape or attempted rape.[17] Younger women seem to be at heightened risk: Adolescents ages 16 to 19 were 3.5 times more likely than the general population to be victims of rape, attempted rape, or sexual assault.[18]

As with other forms of violence against women, rape is highly underreported. With the police notified in only about one in six such cases, rape is among the country's most underreported violent crimes. Fully 84 percent of rape victims, according to one study, had not reported the rape to the police.[19]

The psychological consequences of this form of sexual assault can be as serious as those resulting from domestic violence. Thirty-one percent of all rape victims develop rape-related posttraumatic stress disorder,[20] and rape victims are three times more likely than nonvictims to experience a major depressive episode in their lives. The rate of suicide attempts by rape victims is 13 times higher than among nonvictims, and women who have been raped are 10 times more likely to use illegal substances or alcohol.[21]

While even less well documented, sexual harassment, stalking, and exploitative involvement in the sex industry are also understood to be serious, common, and threatening problems that have significant physical, emotional, and social consequences for women.[22]

Patterns of violence

While the various forms of violence against women are often studied separately, evidence suggests a strong relationship among them. For example, 78 percent of rapes are committed by someone known to the victim.[23] The extent to which being in an intimate relationship affects the nature of abuse was confirmed in a study that indicated 82 percent of women raped or sexually assaulted by a lone offender were victimized by a spouse, ex-spouse, partner, friend, acquaintance, or relative, and 26 percent of all rapes and sexual assaults against women were committed by an intimate partner.[24] Several studies have shown that marital rape is often more violent and repetitive than other forms of this crime and is less commonly reported.[25] Taken together, the aggregate picture of violence against women presents a compelling call to action for researchers, policymakers, and practitioners.[26]

Data limitations

Many researchers concur that because violence against women is seriously underreported and because most quantitative studies focus on only one dimension of the issue, new research is needed.[27] First, few studies have explored the aggregate picture or intersection of the various forms of abuse, even though evidence shows there may be "overlap." Second, because most quantitative research is bound by predetermined or researcher-driven categories, it cannot capture the nuanced pattern of experiences or the types of violence to which different groups of women are subjected.[28] Finally, the need for empirical research on violence against women is particularly acute with regard to women whose experiences with violence fall outside the dominant paradigms that have framed the studies cited here.[29] While ample evidence suggests that violence against women is a problem for all segments of society, the experiences of certain groups of women are virtually unrepresented in the current body of research.

Women involved in illegal activity: An understudied group

One group that has not been adequately studied consists of women involved in illegal activity. When they have been victimized by violence, they may be reluctant to call the police, report abuse to other agencies, or use mainstream social services because of their marginalized social position and precarious legal status.[30] Research on workplace violence, for example, does not include such places of illegal employment as the sites of drug trafficking. Similarly, women involved in prostitution or otherwise working in the sex industry are less likely to report having been raped by a customer or stalked by a pimp. Young women who are truant do not appear in data on victimization gathered in schools, and if a woman is hurt by her partner in crime during a robbery or is sexually harassed in a place where stolen goods are taken, there is little likelihood that her experience with violence will appear in official reports or research findings.

The need documented

Until recently, very little research had been conducted on violence against this group of women. What data had been collected, largely by advocacy groups, suggested that violence is a major factor in the lives of women who are currently in correctional facilities. For example, a 1996 survey of incarcerated women found that at least half of all female prisoners had experienced some form of sexual abuse before their imprisonment.[31]

Recently, BJS studied violence committed against women involved in illegal activity.[32] The study, which confirmed the need for further research, indicates a similar figure—almost half of all women in jails and prisons had been physically or sexually abused before their imprisonment—a much higher rate than reported for the overall population. Also, the study reports significant rates of drug and alcohol use among abused women in State prisons. Nearly 70 percent of the abused women serving time in correctional facilities said they used illegal drugs during the month before their current offense compared with 54 percent of the women who had not been abused. The National Clearinghouse for the Defense of Battered Women, one of the few national organizations that collect data on the relationship between violence against women and women's involvement in illegal activity, reports that more than half of all women in detention had been battered or raped before being incarcerated.[33]

Previously, the most comprehensive documentation of violence against women involved in illegal activity was reports of hearings conducted in 1985 at the Bedford Hills Correctional Facility in New York State. The Bedford Hills study established that many incarcerated women shared the experience of previous domestic and sexual violence and that the abuse they suffered was serious.[34] Findings of a comprehensive followup study indicate that more than 80 percent of the women incarcerated in that same facility 10 years later had a much higher rate of past abuse and that the abuse was much more significant and traumatic.[35]

A study that served as the empirical basis for this paper reported that 40 percent of women in a large urban jail had experienced violence at the hands of an intimate partner, and 35 percent reported sexual abuse.[36] The researcher followed up the study with a qualitative research project that revealed a complex relationship between previous intimate victimization, women's involvement in illegal activity, and the experiences of violence within this understudied group.[37]

In and of itself, documentation of the higher rates of physical and sexual abuse of incarcerated women is important. However, this discussion attempts to transcend the well-known rate differentials to focus on the nature, impact, and relationships among various forms of violence in the lives of women in precarious legal circumstances. Furthermore, it argues that violence in some women's lives may actually contribute to their involvement in illegal activity and that domestic violence or sexual victimization may be related to women's abuse while in custody. Although research has found a relatively high rate of previous domestic or sexual violence in the histories of women involved in illegal activity, only a few discussions have explored a possible causal relationship or covariance between abuse in the private sphere, victimization in the criminal arena, and illegal activity. Perhaps this is more than simply a gap in the research; it is a significant theoretical and conceptual oversight that may seriously limit the understanding of and response to the problem of violence against women in this country, especially against women who are most marginalized and most at risk.

The context: Women in the criminal justice system

The overall context of this broader understanding of the problem of violence against women is established through data on women in the criminal justice system. Currently, about 138,000 women are in jails or prisons in the United States. This figure represents a tripling of the number of incarcerated women between 1985 and 1997.[38] While their absolute numbers are much smaller than those of their male counterparts, the annual rate of increase is significantly higher for women: On average, the female prison population grew more than 11 percent annually since 1985, while the male prison population grew 8 percent at the same time.[39] This precipitous increase is tentatively attributed to a change in both arrest policies and crime patterns.[40] Most criminologists take these changes seriously and are interested in exploring their underlying causes.[41]

Gender and race

Related issues for criminologists include the patterns of women's illegal behavior. Overwhelmingly, women are incarcerated for nonviolent offenses, primarily for violating laws that prohibit the sale and possession of specific drugs.[42] Some investigators have argued that this pattern of illegal behavior is decidedly gender related—that drug sales and other nonviolent crimes are "survival crimes" that women commit to earn money, feed a drug-dependent habit, or escape terrifying intimate relationships and brutal social conditions.[43] Incarcerated women typically have a history of unmet social, educational, health, and economic needs, in addition to a history of victimization.[44] Taken together, these factors indicate the population of incarcerated women to be of heightened significance to family and sexual violence researchers interested in expanding knowledge about violence against women.

Incarcerated women are disproportionately women of color (particularly black and Hispanic/Latina) from low-income communities who have been subjected to a disproportionately high rate of violence.[45] This overrepresentation creates an additional opportunity for researchers. Until now, violence against women of color and against women in low-income communities and their involvement in illegal activity have been considered independently, and few researchers have attempted a more focused exploration of the covariance of these variables. Further, as previously noted, studies that use quantitative methods to determine rates of violence against women have not included illegal behavior as one of the items explored.[46] While violence against women has been established as a serious problem, and although the rapidly increasing rate of incarceration of women in this country is a grave concern, virtually no scholarly work has attempted to link the two. The following public policy and programmatic recommendations seek to respond to this gap.

Public policy and programmatic recommendations

Criminologists and others who study violence against women have been calling for analyses of difficult-to-reach populations and studies of the relationships between various forms of violence against women.[47] An example of such a population is the women who are most marginalized (such as women involved in crime, who are typically women of color from low-income communities, many of whom have substance abuse problems) who are vulnerable to both abuse and crime.

Important considerations challenge the work of several communities of practitioners. Domestic violence advocates and sexual assault service providers need new information about the effects of abuse against women and the ways in which abuse influences women's participation in illegal activity. Practitioners also need a revised analytical framework upon which to base a new set of intervention strategies for reducing violence against women.

Those who design programs to address the needs of incarcerated women or women at risk of arrest would do well to consider the correlation between violence against women and their involvement in crime. Prison-based programming, which is in dire need of gender-specific approaches, would benefit in particular. Such emphasis is consistent with the current interest in addressing the concrete needs of women while they are incarcerated, preparing them to make life changes once they are released.[48]

The National Institute of Justice, other Federal agencies, criminologists, and advocates for incarcerated women and female ex-prisoners are looking for ways to improve the reentry process and decrease recidivism.[49] Considerable attention is being paid to minimizing the factors that contribute to rearrest and to strengthening opportunities for women's empowerment and reintegration into society upon release from prison.[50] The development of policy would benefit from the wider, deeper understanding called for in this paper.

Conceptual and methodological advances in violence research would benefit from avoiding dichotomous categorization and turning instead to undertaking research that is free of predetermined categories. Research on previously understudied groups that uses qualitative methods should enhance policy development and intervention strategies by building the knowledge base. Applying the results of this new research may possibly reduce both the rates of violence against women and women's participation in crime.

Notes

1. Dobash, R.E., and R.P. Dobash, *Women, Violence and Social Change*, New York: Routledge, 1992; and National Research Council, *Understanding Violence Against Women*, ed. N.A. Crowell and A.W. Burgess, Washington, DC: National Academy Press, 1996.

2. Greenfeld, Lawrence A., et al., *Violence by Intimates: Analysis of Data on Crimes by Current or Former Spouses, Boyfriends, and Girlfriends*, Factbook, Washington, DC: U.S. Department of Justice, Bureau of Justice Statistics, March 1998 (revised May 1998): 3, NCJ 167237. This figure, which reflects data on women age 12 or older, is based on an average for the period 1992 to 1996. The violent victimizations included murder as well as rape, sexual assault, robbery, and aggravated and simple assault.

3. Tjaden, P., and N. Thoennes, *Prevalence, Incidence, and Consequences of Violence Against Women: Findings From the National Violence Against Women Survey*, Research in Brief, Washington, DC: U.S. Department of Justice, National Institute of Justice, and Centers for Disease Control and Prevention, November 1998: 7, NCJ 172837. The survey, conducted between 1995 and 1996, includes women age 18 and older.

4. Commonwealth Fund, *The Commonwealth Fund Commission on Women's Health: Addressing Domestic Violence and Its Consequences*, New York: Commonwealth Fund, 1998; and Wilt, S., and S. Olson, "Prevalence of Domestic Violence in the United States," *Journal of the American Medical Women's Association* 53 (2) (1996).

5. Straus, M., *Physical Violence in American Families: Risk Factors and Adaptations to Violence in 8,145 Families*, New Brunswick, NJ: Transaction Publishers, 1990.

6. Browne, A., "Violence Against Women: Relevance for Medical Practitioners," *Journal of the American Medical Association* 267 (23) (1992): 3184–3189; and Rand, M.R., and K. Strom, *Violence-Related Injuries Treated in Hospital Emergency Departments*, Washington, DC: U.S. Department of Justice, Bureau of Justice Statistics, 1997.

7. Federal Bureau of Investigation, *Crime in the United States*, Washington, DC: U.S. Department of Justice, Federal Bureau of Investigation, 1995.

8. Tjaden, P., and N. Thoennes, *Stalking in America: Findings From the National Violence Against Women Survey*, Research in Brief, Washington, DC: U.S. Department of Justice, National Institute of Justice, and Centers for Disease Control and Prevention, April 1998: 4–5, NCJ 169592; Hampton, R.L., and R.J. Gelles, "Violence Towards Black Women in a Nationally

Representative Sample of Black Families," *Journal of Comparative Family Studies* 25 (1) (1994): 105–119; and Salomon, A., "Patterns of Welfare Use Among Poor and Homeless Women," *American Journal of Orthopsychiatry* 66 (1996): 510–525.

9. Hutchinson, I.W., J.D. Hirschel, and D.E. Pesackis, "Family Violence and Police Utilization," *Violence and Victims* 9 (4) (1994): 299–313; Richie, B., *Compelled to Crime: The Gender Entrapment of Black Battered Women*, New York: Routledge, 1996; and Sullivan, C.M., and M.H. Rumptz, "Adjustment and Needs of African American Women Who Utilized a Domestic Violence Shelter," *Violence and Victims* 9 (3) (1994): 275–286.

10. Anti-Violence Project/National Coalition of Anti-Violence Programs, *Report on Lesbian, Gay, Bisexual and Transgendered Domestic Violence*, New York: Anti-Violence Project/National Coalition of Anti-Violence Programs, 1998.

11. Renzetti, C., and C. Miley, *Violence in Gay and Lesbian Domestic Partnerships*, New York: Hayworth Press, 1996.

12. Straus, *Physical Violence in American Families*.

13. Doumas, D., G. Margolin, and R.S. John, "The Intergenerational Transmission of Aggression Across Three Generations," *Journal of Family Violence* 9 (1994):157–175.

14. Gelles, R.J., and J.W. Harrop, "Violence, Battering and Psychological Distress Among Women," *Journal of Interpersonal Violence* 4 (4) (1989): 400–420.

15. Stark, E., and A. Flitcraft, *Women at Risk: Domestic Violence and Women's Health*, Thousand Oaks, CA: Sage Publications, 1996.

16. Ringel, Cheryl, *Criminal Victimization 1996: Changes 1995–96 With Trends 1993–96*, Washington, DC: U.S. Department of Justice, Bureau of Justice Statistics, November 1997: 3, NCJ 165812.

17. Tjaden and Thoennes, *Prevalence, Incidence, and Consequences of Violence Against Women*, 3.

18. Ringel, *Criminal Victimization 1996: Changes 1995–96 With Trends 1993–96*, 4.

19. Medical University of South Carolina, *Rape in America: Report to the Nation*, Arlington, VA: National Center for Victims of Crime, 1992.

20. Ibid.

21. Ibid.

22. Miller, J.L., "Prostitution in Contemporary American Society," in *Sexual Coercion: A Sourcebook on Its Nature, Causes, and Prevention*, ed. E. Grauerholz and M.A. Koralewski, New York: Lexington Books, 1991; and Tjaden and Thoennes, *Stalking in America*.

23. Medical University of South Carolina, *Rape in America*.

24. Bachman, R., and L.E. Saltzman, *Violence Against Women: Estimates From the Redesigned Survey*, Washington, DC: U.S. Department of Justice, Bureau of Justice Statistics, 1995, NCJ 154348.

25. Bergen, R.K., "Surviving Wife Rape: How Women Define and Cope With Violence," *Violence Against Women* 1 (2) (1995): 117–138; and Hampton and Gelles, "Violence Towards Black Women," 105–119.

26. Graham, D.L.R., E.I. Rawlings, and R.K. Rigsby, *Loving to Survive: Sexual Terror, Men's Violence, and Women's Lives*, New York: New York University Press, 1994.

27. Hall, P., I. Tessero, and J. Earp, "Women's Experiences With Battering: A Conceptualization From Qualitative Research, *Women's Health Issues* 5 (4) (1995): 173–192; and Reid, P.T., and R. Kelly, "Research on Women of Color: From Ignorance to Awareness," *Psychology of Women Quarterly* 18 (1994): 477–486.

28. Crenshaw, K.W., "Mapping the Margins: Intersectionality, Identity Politics and Violence Against Women of Color," in *The Public Nature of Private Violence*, ed. M.A. Fineman and B. Mykiturk, New York: Routledge, 1994; and Rasche, C.E., "Minority Women and Domestic Violence: The Unique Dilemmas of Battered Women of Color," in *The Criminal Justice System and Women: Offenders, Victims and Workers*, ed. N. Sokoloff and B. Rafel Price, New York: McGraw-Hill, 1995.

29. Kanuha, V., "Domestic Violence, Racism and the Battered Women's Movement in the U.S.," in *Future Interventions With Battered Women and Their Families*, ed. J. Edelson and Z. Eisikovitz, Thousand Oaks, CA: Sage Publications, 1997.

30. Richie, *Compelled to Crime*.

31. Human Rights Watch, *All Too Familiar: Sexual Abuse of Women in U.S. State Prisons*, New Haven: Yale University Press, 1996.

32. Harlow, C.W., *Prior Abuse Reported by Inmates and Probationers*, Washington, DC: U.S. Department of Justice, Bureau of Justice Statistics, 1999, NCJ 172879.

33. Osthoff, S., National Clearinghouse for the Defense of Battered Women, personal communication with author, 1999.

34. New York State Coalition Against Domestic Violence, "Domestic Violence Hearings Held at Bedford Hills Correctional Facility," *New York State Coalition Against Domestic Violence Newsletter*, April 1985.

35. Browne, A., Harvard University, personal communication with author, 1999.

36. Richie, B., and C. Johnson, "Gender Violence, Incarceration and Women's Health: The Prevalence of Abuse History Among Newly Incarcerated Women in a New York City Jail," *Journal of the American Medical Women's Association* 53 (2) (1996): 89–93.

37. Richie, *Compelled to Crime.*

38. *Correctional Populations in the United States, 1995*, Washington, DC: U.S. Department of Justice, Bureau of Justice Statistics, June 1996: 7, NCJ 163916; and Gilliard, Darrel K., and Allen J. Beck, *Prison and Jail Inmates at Midyear 1997*, Bulletin, Washington, DC: U.S. Department of Justice, Bureau of Justice Statistics, January 1998: 4, NCJ 167247.

39. Mumola, C.J., and Beck, A.J., *Prisoners in 1996*, Washington, DC: U.S. Department of Justice, Bureau of Justice Statistics, June 1997: 5, NCJ 164619. In *Prison and Jail Inmates at Midyear 1997*, Gilliard and Beck note the average annual increase in the jail population was 10 percent for women and 6 percent for men (page 6).

40. Bush-Baskette, S., "The War on Drugs as a War Against Black Women," in *Crime Control and Women: Feminist Implications of Criminal Justice Policy*, ed. S.L. Miller, Thousand Oaks, CA: Sage Publications, 1998.

41. Belknap, J., *The Invisible Women: Gender, Crime and Justice*, Belmont, CA: Wadsworth, 1996; and Chesney-Lind, M., *The Female Offender*, Thousand Oaks, CA: Sage Publications, 1997.

42. Mumola and Beck, *Prisoners in 1996.*

43. Richie, *Compelled to Crime*; and Owen, B., *In the Mix: Struggle and Survival in a Women's Prison*, Albany: SUNY Press, 1998.

44. Freudenberg, N., I. Wilets, and M. Greene, "Linking Women in Jail to Community Services: Factors Associated With Rearrest and Retention of Drug-Using Women Following Release From Jail," *Journal of the American Medical Women's Association* 53 (2) (1998): 89–93.

45. Mumola and Beck, *Prisoners in 1996*.

46. Frisch, L.A., "Research That Succeeds, Policies That Fail," *Journal of Criminal Law and Criminology* 83 (1992): 209–216.

47. National Research Council, *Understanding Violence Against Women*.

48. Morash, M., T.S. Bynum, and B.A. Koons, *Women Offenders: Programming Needs and Promising Approaches*, Research in Brief, Washington, DC: U.S. Department of Justice, National Institute of Justice, 1998, NCJ 171668; and Illinois Department of Corrections, *Five Year Plan for Female Inmates*, Springfield, IL: Illinois Department of Corrections, Planning and Research Unit, 1995.

49. U.S. Department of Justice, National Institute of Justice, *Re-entry Courts: Managing the Transition From Prisons to Community, Call for Concept Papers*, Washington, DC: U.S. Department of Justice, National Institute of Justice, 1999.

50. Richie, *Compelled to Crime*.

One Judicial Perspective on the Sex Trade

Kay Tsenin, Judge, Superior Court of San Francisco

A woman appears before me on her eighth bench warrant for failure to appear. She has worn orange jail uniforms for all her court appearances. I greet her by name, and she flashes a grin from ear to ear. I say, "Sunny! You're in custody again—after you promised me last time you would voluntarily come back to court if I released you." She leans forward on the podium and, with a wide grin, says, "I know, Judge. I'm sorry. I lied." I say to her, "Well, you know, Sunny, this time I will have to keep you in custody." She replies, "Sure, Judge, I know." I hope she will remain in custody long enough to agree to participate in a program offering an alternative to incarceration[1]—but not too long, or she will be able to plea, receive credit for time served, and thereby avoid intervention by the justice system to deal with her needs and the causes of her behavior.

Another woman appears, dressed in street clothes. She had been referred to an alternative program but did not show up for the initial interview. The district attorney is arguing vehemently against further such referrals. After all, she has pending cases. I feel she deserves one more chance and, to support my position, point out that at least in the past 6 months she has not picked up any new charges. I tell the defendant we are referring her to pretrial diversion, one of the alternative programs, and she must arrive by 8:30 a.m. In front of the district attorney, and with the court reporter taking down every word, she replies that it will be difficult to wake up so early because she works on the street all night. But, still, she assures me, she will make it there next week.

Another woman appears, dressed in orange; wounds on her face are still crusted with blood. Yet another woman seems to be emaciated and has dark circles under her eyes. Another convulses in front of my bench, and the bailiff looks at me and says, "It's OK, Judge, she's just detoxing." An inmate far more attractive than anyone who has appeared earlier exits the men's holding tank. I look up the prisoner's name in the calendar: Steve Smith. Steve, a transsexual sex worker, beams when

I refer to him as "she." Then a non-English-speaking "john" (or prostitute's customer) stands before me. According to his financial declaration, he has a minimum-wage job. He appears to be dazed and confused about why he is even in court.

My assignment is the misdemeanor criminal calendar, and the women and men I see are charged with violation of section 647(b) of the California Penal Code: "solicitation." Sometimes the women are charged with being public nuisances. Almost always, a charge in their history is related to drug use, often petty theft. It is a virtual certainty that, without intervention, there soon will be a felony charge involving drugs.

The sex workers who stand before me every day are victims as well as defendants. The johns simply do not understand why they are in a criminal court when, in their eyes, they are merely exercising their male prerogative of sex on demand. These men seem to be unaware of their role in promoting the sex industry.

Judicial officers are sworn to uphold and enforce the law. Most also feel a moral obligation to somehow make the city a better place. We would like to believe that we are agents of change for the better, not simply automatons applying rules and laws to the case patterns that appear before us. This area of the law—dealing with the sex trade—affords a great opportunity to bring about change and to be creative in dealing with people whose conduct is defined by the legislature as criminal but who are victims themselves—and often victimized over and over again.

Judicial approaches

Two judicial approaches are used to handle issues of the so-called oldest profession—that is, solicitation, prostitution, and sex trade street workers, or "B" cases.[2] The first, and more traditional, approach is simply to enforce the law and sentence offenders to county jail or the sheriff's work program. That is easy and simple—virtually a "no-brainer." The message is clear: You commit the crime, you do the time. This approach, however, fails to address the core issues, virtually guarantees recidivism, and does little to change or eliminate prostitution. In addition, a conviction is often difficult, if not impossible, to obtain because juries think such cases waste time and society's judicial resources.

The second approach is for the court to become involved in devising solutions on a case-by-case basis. To accomplish this, one must understand the dynamics. The victim-perpetrator status of the defendant is only one of numerous contradictions. Everyone touched by the problem—homeowners, merchants, law enforcement officers, judicial staff, and even the sex worker—operates in an environment of conflicting attitudes. Consider the homeowner who wants the street worker off his or her block but will rarely vote to convict when serving on a jury. Or the street worker, both victim and defendant, who wants to "get out of the life" and, at the same time, finds that she not only is lured back by the promise of love, security, and happiness but also is dependent on it for survival. All too often, she returns to the street because it is simply the only means of survival available to her.

The sex worker: Victim and survivor

Sex trade workers come in all ages, sizes, and races. One can only wonder why people "choose" this life. What did they look like in their first-grade school pictures? What happened to their dreams and hopes? Most women enter the sex trade as a survival strategy. At some point in their lives, most sex workers have faced a crisis, either social or economic, that compelled them to leave their "conventional" lives behind.

Sex workers are victims and also survivors, often of childhood sexual abuse or abuse by husbands, boyfriends, or pimps. Numerous studies have shown that approximately 90 percent of women in the sex trade have been battered by a member of their family, and more than 70 percent have been sexually abused between the ages of 3 and 14.[3] A young woman running away from abuse will market the one commodity she knows sells: sex. On average, a woman is 14 years of age when she turns to prostitution.

In San Francisco, a recent study by Melissa Farley of 130 prostitutes showed that 68 percent had been repeatedly raped.[4] These individuals are survivors of a society that teaches women from the time they are very young that their sexuality is a commodity—and they may use it to convince someone to do them a favor, avoid a speeding ticket, or get a date to the junior prom. The media and popular culture continually display images of women as sexual commodities and use sex to sell products from shoe polish to CDs, cars, and cigarettes. Then why not sell sex, these women conclude, if that is all you have to support yourself, your children, your boyfriend, and, all too often, your drug habit.

Many women in the sex trade are also survivors of poverty, which affects men and women differently. More than one-third of all households in the United States are headed by women. Even today, women often lack access to the training, jobs, and pay men receive.[5] Even more important, girls who are sexually abused—and 75 percent to 95 percent of 14- to 18-year-old girls in the justice system have been victims of abuse—suffer from a traumatic and profound lack of self-esteem. These girls engage in disempowering and self-defeating behaviors, which propel them into a cycle of prostitution, addiction, drug dealing, and violence. Typically having never received the valuable life-skills training that a healthful family environment provides, these girls see violence and sexual exploitation as the norm. They have never known responsible, respectful, and caring adults and peers; they have never learned how to form durable relationships based on mutual support and affection. Without trust and healthy self-esteem, neither the girls nor the women they become can even use the support systems that are available. That is where the courts come in—and that is where judicial officers can provide the impetus and monitoring necessary for interventions to take place.

More than "quality of life"

In decades past, solicitation was considered a victimless crime. In the 1990s, it was transformed into a quality-of-life crime (that is, a crime that is not wrong in itself but that interferes with the quality of life of other people—merchants, tourists, and neighbors). In reality, no matter how supportive people may be of sex workers, they do not want to witness solicitation in front of their homes, on their street corners, or in front of their neighborhood restaurants.

Prostitution is *not* a victimless crime—the primary victim is the prostitute. And prostitution is much more serious than quality-of-life crimes. Bench officers have the choice of revictimizing the victim or providing that individual with the motivation, incentive, and, sometimes, the courage to change.

Alternative programs, such as Standing Against Global Exploitation (SAGE), a counseling and outreach organization launched in San Francisco in 1995; and Promise, a peer counseling group (described at the conclusion of this paper), offer some first steps in the right direction. The special value of these programs is that survivors of the sex trade run them. It is a well-documented fact that the priorities economically disadvantaged people set for themselves often are not the same priorities set by policymakers, and the same is true for sex workers. Therefore, alternative programs run by peer counselors who know and understand prostitutes' priorities are most effective. These programs offer the experiential perspective, support, and tools needed for participants to succeed, and court officials can provide the impetus. It must be understood, however, that women do not become prostitutes in a few days, weeks, or months. Therefore, getting out of prostitution—like quitting drugs or alcohol—does not happen in a single session, week, or month, and often does not occur without relapse.

Courts and the communities they serve: Contradictions and ambivalence

Courts do not and cannot function in a vacuum. Whether or not they want to, they often mirror community values. Laws prohibiting solicitation—the exchange of money for sex—are enacted and enforced in a sea of contradictions and ambivalence. Judicial officers, whose role is not only to enforce the law but also to ensure that justice is served and to reduce or prevent the likelihood of recidivism, need to be aware of these contextual issues.

Solicitation versus "charity" sex

On one hand, laws on the books proscribe the exchange of sex for money; on the other hand, every day some women have sex because men are nice to them, take them out to dinner, give them gifts, or provide shelter or status. Sex after receipt of a benefit is not a crime as long as it is given without a prior bargain. The key is to not solicit the sex, at least overtly. So charity sex, as it is sometimes called, is very much part of our society. However, to solicit sex for a reward before the reward is given is a crime.

The sex trade is glamorized in songs: "Fancy" escapes poverty and death and attains riches because she follows her mother's advice to be "nice to the men" and, as her mother predicted, the men are "nice to her." Is Fancy a whore or is she participating in charity sex? Is it that women can be grateful but cannot be demanding? Does legality depend on whether the bargain is struck before sex, or does it depend on whether the woman pretends she is doing it for free? *Irma La Douce, Sweet Charity, Pretty Woman*—we romanticize the sweet, vulnerable, poignant sex worker who finds the right man and moves to the house with the white picket fence. These stories are no truer than *Jack and the Beanstalk* or *Hansel and Gretel*, and no more likely than Ed McMahon sending you $1 million in the mail.

Two classes of sex workers, two classes of customers

The enforcement of prostitution laws is also ambivalent. There are two classes of sex workers: the street worker and the call girl. There are also two classes of customers: the street john and the john who can afford high-priced call girls. And, of course, there is the pimp or the trader. Although street workers appear on my calendar every day, not one call girl or one high-priced john has ever stood before me during all my years on the bench. Nor could any of the colleagues I asked at the Hall of Justice recall when a pimp actually appeared before them, charged with a crime. Arrests are directed toward those who can solicit only $20 to $40 for a "half-and-half" (half oral and half more conventional sex) and toward those who can afford to pay no more than that.

Public pressure

The rise and fall of arrests for solicitation depend largely on public pressure. The same people who tell the courts, when they are on a jury, that we should not be spending time on solicitation turn around and join their neighbors in cries to get sex workers off street corners. When a neighborhood pressures the police or elected officials to clean up the street corners, the number of cases increases. Neighborhood residents say they don't want prostitution on their blocks, and they also don't think solicitation laws should be criminally enforced; yet, they want the police and the district attorney to do something. Mandated intervention programs are a major part of the solution. In enforcing laws against solicitation, we are protecting the communities from the nuisance of solicitation and, at the same time—acting in loco parentis—protecting the street worker from herself, her pimp, and the ravages of her work. Melissa Farley's study of prostitutes revealed that 82 percent of them said they had been assaulted by customers, 88 percent had been physically threatened, and 83 percent had been threatened with a weapon.[6]

The issue of jury nullification also comes into play. It is extremely difficult to obtain a conviction in solicitation cases because the jurors feel that consensual conduct between two adults should not be legislated or enforced and that their tax dollars should not be spent trying these cases—unless, of course, the conduct occurs on their street corners. And even then, jurors are looking for a noncriminal resolution.

Kay Tsenin, Judge, Superior Court of San Francisco

Feminist issues

Some women make a rational decision to enter this profession without shame and are demanding the right to be recognized without shame. These women rarely are seen in court.

Some feminists argue for decriminalization and unionization of sex workers. Others claim prostitution is a continuation of sexual abuse of women by men. Survivors of prostitution are also divided on the subject. Some argue that it is a crime by men against women—nothing less than the commercialization of sexual abuse and perpetuation of the inequality that women suffer in all other forums, and part of a global traffic in sexual slavery of women. Others demand lawful recognition of prostitution and raising its status to that of a valid, protected occupation.

There are also arguments that prostitution demonstrates a woman's right to control her body; that selling it is free enterprise—in effect, a career choice; and that pimps are, in fact, entrepreneurs.

Conflicting roles

Add to this milieu of contradictions the opposing roles of the district attorney, often reluctantly prosecuting; public defenders, who sometimes take the myopic view that their role is only to free their clients from custody and not to consider what may be in their clients' best interest in the long run; and the courts, with overburdened calendars. All of these players pull in different directions; alternative programs help bring them together toward a solution.

Interventions

If the goal is to dismantle the sex trade industry, we cannot escape the fact that society creates prostitution and the customer fuels the need for it. If we want to take on this lofty task, we would do well to confront these issues and address them. But on the road to achieving that goal, certain interventions would be helpful. These include providing a way out for the prostitutes and educating the johns about their role in perpetuating prostitution and the sex trade industry.

Alternative programs are a great step. Although their effect is currently limited to the participants, they are initiating a discourse that may have long-term and broad-based preventive effects. SAGE, the First Offender

Prostitution Program (FOPP), and other effective programs in San Francisco were started and are run by ex-street workers.

Meeting the needs of sex workers

One broad-based and enterprising effort is the SAGE counseling and outreach organization in San Francisco. The SAGE Trauma and Recovery (STAR) Center addresses the multiple needs of sex workers recovering from drug addiction, prostitution, and trauma through peer counseling and individual therapy, holistic healing, and vocational services. Women enter the program via two routes: court referrals and an extensive outreach program on the street that involves volunteers and police. Court referrals usually are for eight sessions and may be made for either first-time or repeat offenders. Usually, the incentive is that charges will be dismissed upon program completion.

Not all women complete the program on their first, second, or even third attempt. Many are also trying to get off drugs and are dealing with numerous other psychological and survival issues. SAGE offers the services of peer counselors as well as acupuncture, trauma recovery groups, relapse prevention, self-defense training, and yoga.

The SAGE program for teenage girls targets 14- to 18-year-olds, who are usually referred by the court or the probation department. The 15-week program emphasizes education, psychological needs, life skills, and self-esteem issues. Intake assessment is conducted for problems related to depression, posttraumatic stress, and self-esteem, with followup after 6 weeks. SAGE addresses the girls' need to learn to trust responsible, respectful, and caring adults and peers and to learn how to form durable relationships based on mutual support and affection. SAGE also provides assistance and training in life and personal growth skills, including housing assistance, job training and development, financial counseling, and problem solving.

Educating the customers

FOPP is a program based in the San Francisco district attorney's office that offers counseling to prostitutes' customers in an effort to reduce arrests, recidivism, and exploitation of the women.[7] It is designed for first-time johns and facilitated by former prostitutes. Since 1995, approximately 2,700 solicitors of prostitutes have been diverted from the court system and received an educational (and hopefully rehabilitative) experience in lieu of criminal prosecution. After first-time offenders are arrested, usually through undercover decoy operations, they are cited and offered the opportunity to participate in the program instead of being charged and jailed. Men pay a fee (based on a sliding scale up to $500) and attend one 8-hour class that covers the penal risks and practical consequences of continued criminal conduct and educates them about HIV and other sexually transmitted diseases. In addition, prostitution survivors speak about childhood risk factors, violence, drug use, rehabilitation, and reintegration. Other topics include pimping, recruitment, and trafficking tactics used against women and girls; sexual addiction; and domestic violence education that examines power and equality in relationships.

Other programs

Other alternative programs include Sister/Power, Promise, and Safe House. The 12- to 18-week Sister/Power programs feature ongoing groups that use peer counselors and the resources of the adult probation department. These programs address sexual trauma, drug abuse, and life skills. The Sister program serves women in custody, and the Power program is a postrelease group for the women after they leave prison or jail.

The Promise program is operated and staffed by peer counselors who provide transitional housing using vouchers for local hotels. Their approach focuses on the women's financial needs because women often engage in prostitution for financial reasons. Promise emphasizes life skills, job skills, and transitioning.

Safe House, a "clean and sober" residential community for women leaving prostitution, provides 24-hour staffing, clothing, food, and vocational and training assessments. Women can stay for as long as 18 months. If a woman is not clean and sober for at least 6 months before entering, she must participate in a day treatment program. Safe House offers individual and group counseling, referrals to drug treatment, vocational training, domestic violence counseling, and counseling for sexual assault trauma.

These programs are not exclusive; they often work in conjunction with each other. For example, a woman in Safe House may also participate in the SAGE, Promise, or Power program.

Future needs: Resources and self-worth

Needed resources include bilingual education, geared toward both English-speaking and non-English-speaking communities, to inform residents that it is a crime to solicit sex, that johns will be arrested, and that johns' acts have broad consequences and implications. Also needed are interventions for and intensive assistance to victims of child abuse; mobile units providing health care, legal assistance, and other resources to street workers; drop-in or short-term shelters open 24 hours per day offering medical, legal, and other resources; shelters for runaway youths where no questions will be asked and where they will not fear being sent back to their abusers; mental health care facilities; long-term shelters for women and children; access to drug treatment on demand; education for judicial officers; and financial training and places for women to make the transition from the sex trade to a viable alternative career. Although women cannot be expected to shift from working in the sex trade to working in sweatshops or fast-food restaurants, there are industries and training that would be appropriate, plausible, and attractive. Before a woman can participate in these programs, however, she needs to have time and space to heal and regroup.

If we really want to dismantle the sex worker industry, we need to address core issues. Just as we might try to imagine prostitutes when they were in the first grade, we might also wonder about their abusers. Are they enjoying baseball games while, 20 years later, their victims are struggling to live from day to day on the street, suffering from debilitating posttraumatic stress, or self-medicating with illegal drugs? Is the abuser barbecuing this weekend while his victim is confined to a jail cell suffering from suicidal urges and engaging in life-threatening behaviors?

As long as there is sexual abuse of girls, women will continue to grapple with profound and traumatic low self-worth and self-esteem issues. And as long as women's sexuality is treated as a commodity in the media and women lack access to adequate employment, prostitution will exist. As long as men continue to believe that sex on demand is their male prerogative, it will not matter how many street sweeps are conducted or how many arrests are made. The only chance to make things better is to instill a sense of self-worth in all girls at a very early age and to educate young people on many fronts.

We need to stop the sexual abuse of children and provide women in poverty with adequate resources so they will not have to trade sex for survival. We also need to provide meaningful and concrete assistance and resources to sex workers who want to quit. Although we cannot dismantle this system overnight, we can begin.

Notes

1. In San Francisco, numerous programs offer alternatives to incarceration for sex trade workers. Among them are FOPP (First Offender Prostitution Program, for both "johns" and sex workers), SAGE (Standing Against Global Exploitation), and pretrial diversion. Except for the first offender programs, each usually involves a counseling component, frequently substance abuse treatment, and often a needs assessment with an attempt to address the needs.

2. These cases are so called because they involve prostitution charged under section 647(b) of the California Penal Code.

3. Women Hurt in Systems of Prostitution Engaged in Revolt (WHISPER), Oral History Project, Minneapolis, 1988. The Mary Magdalene Project in Reseda, California, reported that 80 percent of the women they worked with were sexually abused as children. Genesis House in Chicago reported that 94 percent of the women they worked with were abused as children. These reports were made at the First National Workshop for Those Working with Female Prostitutes, Wayzata, Minnesota, 1985.

4. Farley, Melissa, and Howard Barkan, "Prostitution, Violence Against Women, and Posttraumatic Stress Disorder," *Women & Health* 27 (3) (1998): 37–49. Dr. Farley works with Prostitution Research & Education, a project sponsored by San Francisco Women's Centers.

5. Although men and women engage in this work for many of the same reasons, male sex workers have even fewer resources. However, male sex workers and the international sex trade are beyond the scope of this paper.

6. Farley and Barkan, "Prostitution, Violence Against Women, and Posttraumatic Stress Disorder."

7. The First Offender Prostitution Program was among the winners of the prestigious Innovations in American Government awards competition in 1998.

Childhood Victimization and the Derailment of Girls and Women to the Criminal Justice System

Cathy Spatz Widom, Ph.D., University of Medicine and Dentistry of New Jersey

There has been a general perception that we do not need to understand, or intervene to prevent, female delinquent or criminal behavior because small numbers of women are involved, such offenses are primarily sexual in nature, and the female offender is the exception—a manifestation of extreme forms of psychological deviance. Early researchers have referred to female offenders as "themselves on the whole a sorry lot,"[1] focused on their "precocious sexual development" as the root cause of their delinquency,[2] and described the criminal woman as "a monster . . . whose wickedness must have been enormous before it could triumph over so many obstacles."[3] Others have described the female offender as relatively nonthreatening to society: "The girls and women who make up the bulk of the criminal justice workload involving the female offender (and are the grist of the female offender programs) commit ordinary crimes—mostly minor thefts and frauds, low level drug dealing, prostitution, and simple assaults involving their mates or children. . . . They are *not* career criminals" (emphasis added).[4]

In reality, the problem of female criminality is substantially more complex than presented in the literature—and girls and women may be the victims as well as the offenders. It is tempting to conclude from reports describing the extent of childhood sexual and physical abuse and neglect in the backgrounds of incarcerated women that their childhood victimization experiences have somehow played a role in their offending.[5] A better way to answer questions about the role of childhood victimization in the development of criminal behavior, however, is through prospective longitudinal studies that follow a group of abused and neglected girls into adulthood. These studies allow researchers to identify the proportion of girls who go on to become offenders as adults, learn about their criminal careers, and determine what happens to other abused and neglected girls who might not have experienced such negative outcomes. Previously, most large longitudinal studies providing information for criminologists have involved males, usually white males. Fortunately, some current studies that include young girls will be able to redress some of the earlier study limitations when their subjects grow into adulthood.

The research described in this paper involves a large group of physically and sexually abused and neglected girls and boys (ages 0 to 11) and a matched control group (ages 0 to 11) who were followed and studied into young adulthood. Their criminal histories were gathered when the subjects were approximately 26 years old and again when their average age was about 33.[6] Thus, the subjects had ample opportunity to engage in behavior resulting in arrest.

The study sample represents documented court cases of abuse and neglect. It is important to note that these cases are generally skewed toward the lower end of the socioeconomic spectrum. Therefore, the study findings cannot be generalized to middle- or upper-class cases of abuse and neglect or to cases that do not come to the attention of the authorities—and the consequences may be different for these girls. This paper addresses questions about the role of childhood victimization in the development of female criminal behavior, suggests potential mechanisms in the derailment of girls and women to the criminal justice system, and describes opportunities for intervention.

Role of childhood victimization in the development of criminal behavior

Considering whether childhood victimization derails the normal developmental processes of girls and young women and whether this derailment affects their ability to cope with the demands of life and adulthood involves four key questions:

- Is criminal behavior among abused and neglected girls and women rare?

- Is criminal behavior among abused and neglected girls and women predominantly sexual?

- Do abused and neglected status offenders escalate to criminal offending?
- Do abused and neglected girls develop antisocial or delinquent lifestyles that persist into adulthood as serious criminal careers?

Is criminal behavior among abused and neglected girls and women rare?

When compared with girls who have not been abused and neglected during childhood, abused and neglected girls are nearly twice as likely to be arrested as juveniles (20.0 percent versus 11.4 percent), twice as likely to be arrested as adults (28.5 percent versus 15.9 percent), and 2.4 times more likely to be arrested for violent crimes (8.2 percent versus 3.6 percent). Data also indicate that physical and sexual abuse and neglect lead to increased risk of arrest for violence among women, a pattern *dissimilar* to that identified for abused and neglected males.[7] Although abused and neglected females are at increased risk, however, these relationships are not inevitable or deterministic; about 70 percent do not become offenders.[8]

Is criminal behavior among abused and neglected girls and women predominantly sexual?

While arrests and self-reports indicate that abused and neglected females are at increased risk for prostitution,[9] they also engage in a variety of other criminal behaviors. Of the females in the study sample, 248 were arrested as juveniles or adults, and only 40 (16.1 percent) of these were arrested for prostitution or other sex-related crimes. The remainder were arrested for a variety of other crimes. Interestingly, the majority of the 40 females arrested for sex crimes had been abused or neglected (that is, not the control females).

Do abused and neglected status offenders escalate to criminal offending?

Despite the belief that status offenders do not escalate in their criminal behavior and we should not intervene in their lives,[10] results of this study indicate that they do escalate. About half (49 percent) of the abused and neglected girls who committed status offenses (were arrested as juveniles for an offense that would not be considered criminal if committed by an adult) were arrested as adults as well as 36 percent of the control females. Thus, in both groups, a substantial portion of the girls with status offenses as juveniles were arrested as adults.

Do abused and neglected girls develop antisocial or delinquent lifestyles that persist into adulthood as serious criminal careers?

Peter Lambert, Daniel Nagin, and I have examined developmental trajectories of offending among this sample of individuals. The results of our work challenge the prevailing assumption that female offenders are *not* career criminals. We found a subset of abused and neglected females who develop antisocial and delinquent lifestyles that persist into adulthood and who become "high-rate chronic" or "persistent" offenders with serious criminal careers. This group (about 8 percent of the abused and neglected females in our sample) does not appear among the control females; showed peaks of offending at about ages 26 to 27; and averaged slightly more than one arrest every 2 years (0.6 per year) through age 35. About 38 percent had been picked up for status offenses as girls, but about 54 percent were arrested for property crimes, 76 percent for order offenses, 46 percent for violence, and 32 percent for drug offenses. The overall criminal histories of this group were similar to those of "mid-rate chronic" male offenders.[11]

Mechanisms in derailment

Potential mechanisms in the derailment of girls and women include running away, deficits in cognitive ability and achievement, growing up without traditional social controls, engaging in relationships with deviant or delinquent individuals, and failing to learn the social and psychological skills necessary for successful adult development. Such mechanisms may also offer opportunities for intervention.

Runaways

Researchers have argued that victimization triggers girls' entry into delinquency as they try to escape abusive environments.[12] Adolescent females who are unable to end abuse through legal channels often run away and end up on the streets with few legitimate survival options:

> [They are] unable to enroll in school or take a job to support themselves because they fear detection. . . . [T]hey engage in panhandling, petty theft, and occasional prostitution in order to survive. Young women in conflict with parents (often for very

legitimate reasons) may actually be forced by present laws into petty criminal activity, prostitution, and drug use.[13]

While abused and neglected children are at increased risk for running away, and running away is associated with increased risk of arrest among juveniles and adults, the effect of running away is also seen in nonabused and nonneglected children. Indeed, the increased risk of arrest among control runaways was *higher* than that observed among abused and neglected children, even though the abused and neglected children were already at high risk for criminal behavior.[14]

Neglected young children, alone on the streets, are at risk of being victimized or enticed into prostitution. Runaways may fall under the control of pornographers and pimps and experience subsequent physical and sexual victimization by pimps and customers. Given their lack of adequate medical care and high prevalence of risky lifestyles (which may include prostitution, alcohol, drugs, and smoking), children who run away also may be at risk for multiple problems, including serious public health concerns.

Deficits in IQ or cognitive ability

Abused and neglected women earn lower average scores on IQ tests and tests of reading ability than nonabused and nonneglected women.[15] They are also low achievers scholastically (as evidenced by poor grades, behavioral problems, and expulsion) and complete, on average, one year fewer of school.

We do not know the origin of deficits in academic and intellectual performance among abused and neglected females. The deficits may be caused by brain dysfunction that is a result of brain injury from physical abuse or malnutrition from neglect. Physical abuse (such as battering) or severe neglect (producing, for example, dehydration, diarrhea, or failure to thrive) also may lead to developmental retardation that, in turn, may affect school performance and behavior. Thus, deficits in IQ or cognitive ability resulting from early childhood abuse or neglect may lead to impaired academic performance in elementary or secondary school and decreased cognitive functioning.

Decreased functioning also may result in lowered self-esteem or the lack of a sense of control over one's life, either directly (the child perceives she was somehow responsible for the abuse or neglect or was unable to prevent the victimization) or indirectly (through diminished social and interpersonal skills). Also, because expectations for early academic success are often higher for girls than boys,[16] such deficits in girls may elicit more negative responses from teachers and caregivers that, in turn, may place girls at greater risk for behavioral problems.[17]

Lack of traditional social controls

Traditionally, females are closely supervised, especially during their formative years, and antisocial behavior is discouraged through sanctions. Risk-taking behavior is often discouraged among girls but encouraged and rewarded among boys.[18] Girls' friends are also more carefully monitored, decreasing the likelihood of influence by delinquent peers.[19]

However, the lives of abused and neglected young girls do not necessarily reflect these traditional patterns and social controls. They often grow up in multiproblem homes with alcohol- or drug-abusing parents and other social maladies, lacking the barriers described earlier as holding the normal woman to the path of virtue.[20] Perhaps the "lucky" abused and neglected girls are those who are placed into foster care and bond with foster parents at an early age or those whose grandparents or other relatives are able to rear them successfully.

Relationships with deviant or delinquent friends and relatives

Abused and neglected individuals are more likely to report that someone in their family was arrested (a parent or sibling, for example) than are nonabused and nonneglected individuals. High rates of psychopathology are reported among the families of female delinquents and felons,[21] and antisocial women and men often engage in "assortative" mating (nonrandom mating resulting from the selection of similar partners).[22]

If behavioral preferences are a function of the networks in which a person is embedded,[23] then it would not be surprising that abused and neglected girls and women engaged in deviant or criminal behaviors because their networks offered models or support for such behavior. Since many abused and neglected girls are more likely to grow up in "criminogenic" homes and in neighborhoods with high rates of crime and violence, there may be numerous opportunities for them to learn and model aggressive and antisocial behavior. This picture contrasts sharply with explanations typically offered to explain the generally low rates of female crime. For abused and neglected girls, we need to rethink these models.

Failure to learn social and psychological skills

Finally, childhood victimization may prevent girls from learning the social and psychological skills needed for successful adult development. Abused and neglected girls and women have multiple problems—including lower academic and intellectual performance, more stressful life events,[24] more suicide attempts,[25] increased likelihood of abusing alcohol,[26] higher levels of hostility and sensation seeking, and lower levels of self-esteem and sense of control[27]—than do nonabused and nonneglected girls and women.

Some researchers suggest that the patterns of problems experienced by women lead to noncriminal forms of coping that are not likely to trigger aggressive forms of criminal behavior.[28] Our findings, however, suggest otherwise: Abused and neglected females are more likely to use alcohol and other drugs and turn to criminal and violent behaviors when coping with stressful life events.[29]

The female criminal: Opportunities for intervention

The common explanations for female crime and its nonthreatening nature do not account for the derailment of abused and neglected girls and women to criminal behavior. From a public health perspective, these consequences are particularly important because of the risk of sexually transmitted diseases and the potential of these consequences to facilitate girls' transition into prostitution.

As indicated, about 8 percent of abused and neglected girls (roughly the same proportion as among nonabused and nonneglected males identified in other studies) become chronic, persistent offenders, engaging in violence and other forms of troublesome behavior that persist into adulthood. More research on female offenders in general, and on abused *and* neglected females in particular, is needed because there is very little knowledge about how best to intervene and treat them. Rather than denying there are women who are serious offenders, we need to understand and respond to the mechanisms that lead them to engage in criminal behavior not traditionally associated with women.

Women play a unique role in society: They produce children (80 to 85 percent of the females in this study were mothers). The behavior and health risks (alcohol consumption, for example) these young adult women face are of particular concern—especially because the environments they create will affect the physical and psychosocial development of their children.

We need to pay more attention and intervene when children first come in contact with the criminal justice system as runaways and status offenders, particularly with those who do so at very young ages. We also need to identify the aspects of status offenses that suggest they are precursors of adult criminal activity and the least harmful ways to respond so that these behaviors do not persist. These will be the first steps in preventing the derailment of young abused and neglected girls to the criminal justice system and in enhancing their opportunities to lead healthy and successful lives.

Notes

1. Glueck, S., and E. Glueck, *Five Hundred Delinquent Women*, New York: A.A. Knopf, 1934.

2. Smith, A.D., *Women in Prison*, London: Stevens and Sons, 1962.

3. Lombroso, C., and W. Ferrero, *The Female Offender*, London: Fisher Unwin, 1895.

4. Steffensmeier, D., and L. Broidy, "Explaining Female Offending," in *Women, Crime, and Criminal Justice: Contemporary Perspectives*, ed. C.M. Renzetti and L. Goodstein, Los Angeles, CA: Roxbury Publishing Company, in press.

5. Browne, A., B. Miller, and E. Maguin, "Prevalence and Severity of Lifetime Physical and Sexual Victimization Among Incarcerated Women," *International Journal of Law and Psychiatry* 22 (3/4) (1999): 301–322; and Harlow, C.W., *Prior Abuse Reported by Inmates and Probationers*, Special Report, Washington, DC: U.S. Department of Justice, Bureau of Justice Statistics, April 1999, NCJ 172879.

6. Widom, C.S., "The Cycle of Violence," *Science* 244 (1989): 160–166; and Maxfield, M.G., and C.S. Widom, "The Cycle of Violence: Revisited Six Years Later," *Archives of Pediatrics and Adolescent Medicine* 150 (1996): 390–395.

7. Maxfield and Widom, "The Cycle of Violence."

8. Ibid.

9. Abused and neglected males are also at increased risk for prostitution (based on arrests and/or self-reports) compared with control males (14.2 percent versus 8.0 percent, respectively); see Widom, C.S., and J.B. Kuhns, "Childhood Victimization and Subsequent Risk for Promiscuity, Prostitution, and Teenage Pregnancy," *American Journal of Public Health* 86 (11) (November 1996): 1607–1612.

10. Chesney-Lind, M., "Girls' Crime and Woman's Place: Toward a Feminist Model of Female Delinquency," *Crime and Delinquency* 35 (1) (January 1989): 5–29.

11. Widom, C.S., D. Nagin, and P. Lambert, "Does Childhood Victimization Alter Developmental Trajectories of Criminal Careers?" Paper presented to American Society of Criminology, annual meeting, Washington, DC, November 11–14, 1998.

12. Chesney-Lind, M., "Women and Crime: The Female Offender," *Signs* 12 (1986): 78–96; Chesney-Lind, "Girls' Crime and Woman's Place"; and Chesney-Lind, M., and R. Sheldon, *Girls, Delinquency, and Juvenile Justice*, Pacific Grove, CA: Brooks/Cole, 1992.

13. Chesney-Lind, "Girls' Crime and Woman's Place," 24.

14. Kaufman, J., and C.S. Widom, "Childhood Victimization, Running Away, and Delinquency," *Journal of Research in Crime and Delinquency* 36 (4) (November 1999): 347–370.

15. Perez, C.M., and C.S. Widom, "Childhood Victimization and Long-Term Intellectual and Academic Outcomes," *Child Abuse and Neglect* 18 (8) (1994): 617–633.

16. Keenan, K., and D.S. Shaw, "Developmental and Social Influences on Young Girls' Early Problem Behavior," *Psychological Bulletin* 121 (1997): 95–113.

17. Keenan, K., R. Loeber, and S. Green, "Conduct Disorder in Girls: A Review of the Literature," *Clinical Child and Family Psychology Review* 2 (1999): 3–19.

18. Steffensmeier and Broidy, "Explaining Female Offending."

19. Giordano, P., S. Cernkovich, and M. Pugh, "Friendships and Delinquency," *American Journal of Sociology* 91 (1986): 1170–1203.

20. Lombroso and Ferrero, *The Female Offender*.

21. Cloninger, C.R., and S.B. Guze, "Psychiatric Illness in the Families of Female Criminals: A Study of 288 First-Degree Relatives," *British Journal of Psychiatry* 122 (1973): 697–703.

22. Robins, L.N., *Deviant Children Grown Up*, Baltimore: Williams and Wilkins, 1966.

23. Smith-Lovin, L., and J.M. McPherson, "You Are Who You Know: A Network Approach to Gender," in *Theory on Gender/Feminism on Theory*, ed. P. England, New York: Aldine deGruyter, 1993: 223–254.

24. Chavez, J.M., and C.S. Widom, "Childhood Victimization and Substance Abuse: The Role of Stressful Life Events and Coping Strategies," in review, 1999.

25. Widom, C.S., "Childhood Victimization: Early Adversity and Subsequent Psychopathology," in *Adversity, Stress, and Psychopathology*, ed. B.P. Dohrenwend, New York: Oxford University Press, 1998: 81–95.

26. Widom, C.S., T.O. Ireland, and P.J. Glynn, "Alcohol Abuse in Abused and Neglected Children Followed-Up: Are They at Increased Risk?" *Journal of Studies on Alcohol* 56 (1995): 207–217.

27. Widom, C.S., "Motivation and Mechanisms in the 'Cycle of Violence'," in *Nebraska Symposium on Motivation*, vol. 46, ed. D. Hansen, Lincoln, NE: University of Nebraska Press, in press.

28. Broidy, L., and R. Agnew, "Gender and Crime: A General Strain Theory Perspective," *Journal of Research in Crime and Delinquency* 34 (3) (August 1997): 275–306.

29. Chavez and Widom, "Childhood Victimization and Substance Abuse."

About the National Institute of Justice

The National Institute of Justice (NIJ), a component of the Office of Justice Programs, is the research agency of the U.S. Department of Justice. Created by the Omnibus Crime Control and Safe Streets Act of 1968, as amended, NIJ is authorized to support research, evaluation, and demonstration programs, development of technology, and both national and international information dissemination. Specific mandates of the Act direct NIJ to:

- Sponsor special projects and research and development programs that will improve and strengthen the criminal justice system and reduce or prevent crime.
- Conduct national demonstration projects that employ innovative or promising approaches for improving criminal justice.
- Develop new technologies to fight crime and improve criminal justice.
- Evaluate the effectiveness of criminal justice programs and identify programs that promise to be successful if continued or repeated.
- Recommend actions that can be taken by Federal, State, and local governments as well as by private organizations to improve criminal justice.
- Carry out research on criminal behavior.
- Develop new methods of crime prevention and reduction of crime and delinquency.

In recent years, NIJ has greatly expanded its initiatives, the result of the Violent Crime Control and Law Enforcement Act of 1994 (the Crime Act), partnerships with other Federal agencies and private foundations, advances in technology, and a new international focus. Examples of these new initiatives include:

- Exploring key issues in community policing, violence against women, violence within the family, sentencing reforms, and specialized courts such as drug courts.
- Developing dual-use technologies to support national defense and local law enforcement needs.
- Establishing four regional National Law Enforcement and Corrections Technology Centers and a Border Research and Technology Center.
- Strengthening NIJ's links with the international community through participation in the United Nations network of criminological institutes, the U.N. Criminal Justice Information Network, and the NIJ International Center.
- Improving the online capability of NIJ's criminal justice information clearinghouse.
- Establishing the ADAM (Arrestee Drug Abuse Monitoring) program—formerly the Drug Use Forecasting (DUF) program—to increase the number of drug-testing sites and study drug-related crime.

The Institute Director establishes the Institute's objectives, guided by the priorities of the Office of Justice Programs, the Department of Justice, and the needs of the criminal justice field. The Institute actively solicits the views of criminal justice professionals and researchers in the continuing search for answers that inform public policymaking in crime and justice.

To find out more about the National Institute of Justice,
please contact:

National Criminal Justice Reference Service
P.O. Box 6000
Rockville, MD 20849–6000
800–851–3420
e-mail: *askncjrs@ncjrs.org*

To obtain an electronic version of this document, access the NIJ Web site
(*http://www.ojp.usdoj.gov/nij*).

If you have questions, call or e-mail NCJRS.

www.ingramcontent.com/pod-product-compliance
Lightning Source LLC
Chambersburg PA
CBHW051824170526
45167CB00005B/2143